The *hardest* thing
for your competitors
to duplicate
is the most
powerful advantage
you have –
the **MINDS** and *HEARTS*
of your employees.

PASSIONATE PERFORMANCE

**Engaging Minds and Hearts
to Conquer the Competition**

Lee J. Colan

Passionate Performance

Engaging Minds and Hearts
to Conquer the Competition

Inquiries regarding permission for use of the material contained in this book should be addressed to:
CornerStone Leadership Institute
P.O. Box 764087
Dallas, TX 75376
888.789.5323

Printed in the United States of America
ISBN: 0-9746403-4-4

Credits
Consulting and editing   The Baldwin Group, Dallas, TX   info@BaldwinGrp.com
Design, art direction, and production   Back Porch Creative, Plano, TX   info@BackPorchCreative.com

Dedication

To my wife and partner in life, Julie,
who provides the greatest example
of engaging the minds and hearts
of a team – our family.

en·gage

\in-ʹgāj\ verb

to attract and hold interest;
to cause to participate;
to connect or interlock with.

CONTENTS

INTRODUCTION

In today's hyper-competitive market, a burning question for most companies is this: "How can we achieve a *significant* and *sustainable* competitive advantage in order to retain our customers?" After all, keeping existing customers is five times less expensive than finding new ones. That's good business in anyone's book.

Traditional competitive factors like product design, technology and distribution channels are harder to sustain in a super-fast, mega-networked world. In fact, the good old "Four P's of Marketing" – product, price, promotion and placement – are having much less impact for companies competing in today's marketplace.

A fifth "P" – *people* – has become an increasingly important competitive factor. Consider this: About 70% of customers' buying decisions are based on positive human interactions with sales staff. Add to this the fact that 83% of the U.S. gross domestic product comes from services and information which are created and delivered by people. **The bottom line is that people buy from people, not companies.** So, your people – and the performance they deliver – are the defining competitive advantage for your organization.

When people are engaged in their work and feel a deep connection
to it, they deliver Passionate Performance. Passionate Performance
creates satisfied customers, and ultimately, value for the organization.
Think of the times you've gone shopping or to a restaurant and
dealt with service people who were visibly excited to be in their
jobs and to be serving you. Their words jumped out of their hearts
rather than being regurgitated from a script. They probably surprised
you with the extra effort and thoughtfulness they put toward
satisfying your particular needs or questions – and they actually
seemed happy to do it!

Now, consider how you felt when you left these establishments. Did
you buy more than you had planned? Were you likely to return? Did
you recommend these businesses to friends? You probably answered
"Yes" to at least one of these questions. That's the beginning of a
value chain that starts with engaged employees.

Some people are naturally engaged in their work and consistently
deliver Passionate Performance. The most effective leaders learn how
to bring these qualities out in everyone. They invest time, energy
and resources to engage their people because engaged employees
are more likely to:

♦ stay with the organization;

♦ perform at higher levels;

♦ influence others to perform well;

♦ promote the organization externally; and

♦ deliver unparalleled customer service.

When you discover how to actively engage your people to deliver Passionate Performance, you start a powerful and self-reinforcing cycle that builds value for your organization. This creates a *unique, sustainable* competitive advantage. Given enough time and resources, your competitors can replicate your products, distribution channels and technology. However, Passionate Performance cannot be easily duplicated by your competition and creates a rock-solid wall of differentiation between you and the rest of the pack.

This book offers practical strategies to help you engage your employees – their minds *and* hearts. Using these strategies will create a precious and powerful competitive advantage for your organization.

I hope these pages inspire *your* mind and heart with ideas that help you evoke Passionate Performance from your team.

Read, enjoy and engage!

"If your company is going
to put customers first,
then you must put
employees *more* first."

– Tom Peters
Management Consultant
and Author

THE **ANATOMY** OF **PASSIONATE PERFORMANCE**

Passionate Performance

Passionate Performance is achieved when employees are fully engaged – when they demonstrate a **strong, sustained intellectual *and* emotional attachment to their work.**

You will know when employees are demonstrating Passionate Performance because you will feel the enthusiasm and see the results. Your team will have more fun creating better outcomes. They will be fully present at work, in the moment, in the flow. They will perform at higher levels and be motivated to do more. They will feel like kids again – a time when they had fun doing their very best at whatever they were engaged in. In short, **their work will feel like play.**

Can you remember a situation where you felt like this? Maybe it was a special project where everything came together perfectly. Or a team you were on where everyone did what was best for the team, creating a rare synergy. Or a certain cause you volunteered for where you felt like the best of your skills and talents flowed naturally to make a real difference. Most of us can remember a situation like this because it was such a unique experience and left us with such a special feeling. It may have been a lot of work, but we most frequently describe it as "fun." That's because our minds and hearts were fully engaged.

What does Passionate Performance look like? How will you know when your employees are giving it? Look for signs of the big payoff from Passionate Performance: *discretionary effort* – people *choosing* to do more for you. You'll know your employees are giving discretionary effort when they:

- choose to work late to complete a project;

- ask how they can better serve another team member or department;

- inquire about how their actions affect another function or the customer;

- make a connection between their decisions and the company's financial results;

- treat company resources like their own;

- initiate improvements in work methods;

- look beyond their own roles for improvement opportunities; and

- pursue self-development on their own time.

You might think the instances of employees giving Passionate Performance will be few and far between, *but they don't have to be.* You can learn how to orchestrate Passionate Performance every day.

A Gallup poll revealed that only
26% of U.S. employees are
fully engaged at any time.

On the other end of the spectrum,
19% of employees are
actively disengaged, meaning they
intentionally act in ways that
negatively impact their organizations.
The annual cost nationwide to
employ this actively disengaged
group exceeds $300 billion.

Source: *Gallup Management Journal*, March 2001

The Engagement Challenge

As the research highlighted on the prior page indicates, most employees are not engaged at work – their bodies may be there, but their minds and hearts are not. In fact, 74% of employees are either indifferent to their work or actively disengaged.

Just think of the last time you had to deal with service representatives who made it clear they had something better to do than serve you. Unfortunately, most of us don't have to think much farther back than last week to recall such an interaction.

Are disengaged employees a problem in *your* organization? Do your employees complete only what is asked of them and nothing more? Did you know that actively disengaged employees miss an average of 3.5 more days of work per year than engaged employees? Consider some other effects of disengagement:

- increased turnover;
- missed deadlines;
- low morale;
- high burnout rates;
- complacency;
- finger-pointing; and
- lack of accountability and responsibility.

Do you recognize any of these? If you answered "Yes," that's an indication you have an engagement challenge.

Some disengaged employees will choose to leave your team. Even worse, others will stay on the job, just put in time and be destructive. An employee who quits no longer affects your organization; an actively disengaged employee who stays has a toxic effect on your team and your customers.

Does disengagement look like a pretty bleak picture for leaders?
Not at all! **Disengagement is simply the result of unfulfilled
needs.** Nothing fancy here; these are basic human needs that leaders
either forget to, choose not to, or simply don't know how to fulfill.

The good news is that it doesn't cost a dime to engage employees,
and the strategies you need to engage your team are simple. Even
better, the answers and tools are actually right here at your fingertips.
So, let's look at what you can do to win this engagement challenge.

Engaging Minds and Hearts

Management guru Peter Drucker advises leaders
to, "Accept the fact that we have to treat
almost anybody as a volunteer." *Employees as
volunteers* is a useful concept to remind leaders
that they must continually engage their people. Only fully engaged
employees will give you the discretionary effort required for
Passionate Performance. In the era of the volunteer worker, leaders
must engage their employees to elicit discretionary effort from them.
It may sound like pretty heady and heart-wrenching stuff to fully
engage your employees, but there are simple strategies you can use
in your pursuit of Passionate Performance.

The solution to the engagement challenge is found within the minds
and hearts of employees where basic human needs are fulfilled. It's
a simple but powerful formula: **When my needs are fulfilled, I
am engaged and I perform at my peak ability.** When my needs
are met, I'm motivated to help those who meet my needs. When
my needs are *not* met, I'm frustrated, out of control, unfocused,
and disconnected – in a word, disengaged.

We all have these basic human needs, and they have remained the
same amidst the tornado of external change. Times have changed,
and our world has certainly changed, but people have not. In

many organizations today, these basic needs still go unfulfilled. It's up to you as the leader to fulfill them.

To meet these needs, leaders must first see them and acknowledge them. In order to see them, leaders must view their employees as people and not just workers. If you look at your employees as people, you can identify these six basic needs – three intellectual and three emotional:

Intellectual Needs	Emotional Needs
♦ Achievement	♦ Purpose
♦ Autonomy	♦ Intimacy
♦ Mastery	♦ Appreciation

These needs are interdependent. For example, to engage the minds of your employees, you must fulfill *all three* intellectual needs: achievement, autonomy and mastery. The same holds true for the emotional needs. Therefore, achieving Passionate Performance is a two-sided challenge: intellectual *and* emotional. Successful leaders engage both the minds and hearts of their people.

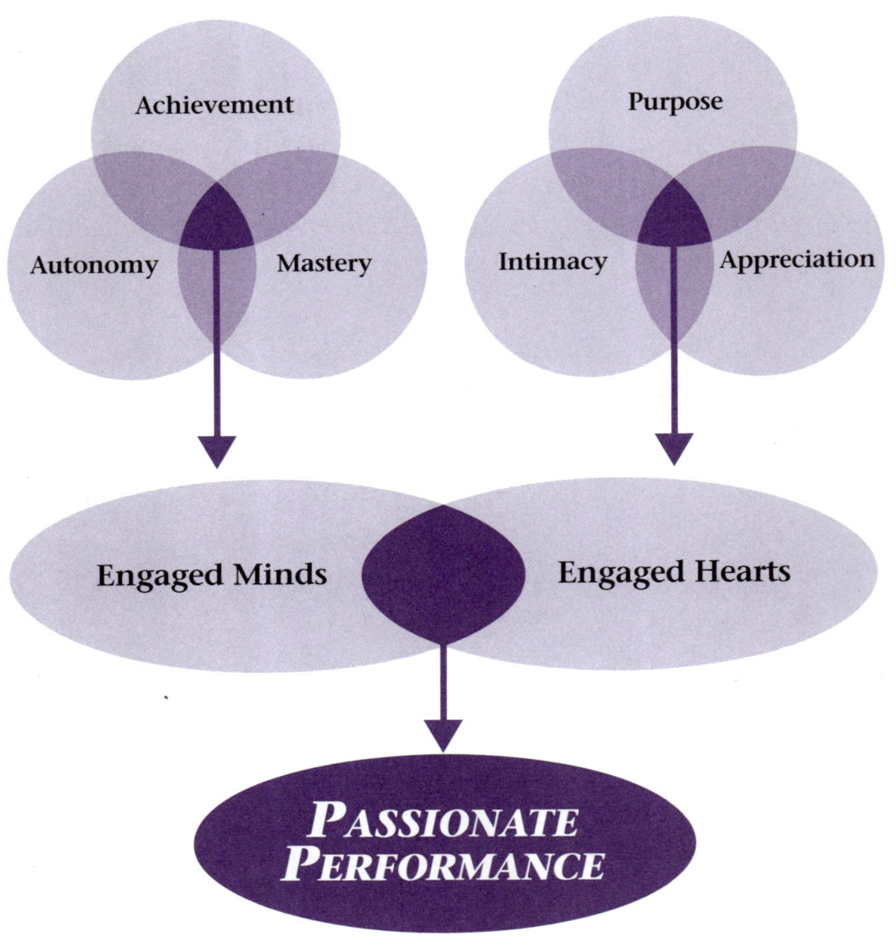

When it comes to Passionate Performance, the mind and the heart go hand in hand. **Engaged minds build your employees' performance and engaged hearts build their passion.** Performance without passion tends to falter during tough times or in the face of challenges that require sacrifice, significant extra effort or unusually creative solutions. On the other hand, passion without performance results in diffused, unfocused efforts.

A close look at great companies reveals a common theme: They have leaders who engage the minds and hearts of their employees and therefore are able to evoke Passionate Performance from their teams. For example, at high-tech giant Agilent, leaders throughout the organization work hard at engaging employees and helping them create strong intellectual and emotional attachments to work. During an economic downturn, the company was forced to eliminate over 8,000 jobs. Because leaders had developed an engaged workforce, they found many laid-off employees working until 10:00 p.m. on their last day just to leave things in good order. Now that's Passionate Performance, and it can shine a light for your organization even during dark times.

How would you like to be able to elicit Passionate Performance from your employees every day? You can if you will take the steps to satisfy their needs. The remaining chapters describe each need and practical strategies you can use to fulfill each one. Although the engagement strategies are simple, make no bones about it – they require lots of hard work. The results will be well worth your effort. Meeting employees' needs builds the foundation for Passionate Performance. When you fulfill their needs, your employees will create a powerful competitive advantage for your organization – guaranteed!

Our newest competitive
advantage is our oldest one –
our employees'
minds and hearts.

"I always felt that my greatest asset was not my physical ability; it was my mental ability."

– Bruce Jenner
Gold Medal Olympic Decathlete

ENGAGING THE MIND

Engaging employees' minds tends to come naturally for many leaders. The mind represents the intellectual aspects of people that are based on reason, logic, and cause and effect. It requires the *science* of leadership which is the focus of most leadership training and education. **Engaging the mind builds employee performance.**

Elevating employees' performance by engaging their minds involves the basics of leadership, but the basics are often overlooked. Even the best professional athletes can lose sight of the basic skills of their sports: An all-star wide receiver takes his eyes off the ball and misses an easy touchdown pass. An Olympic downhill skier doesn't stay in a tight tuck, catches a draft and eats snow. A world-class golfer forgets to shift her weight during a tee shot and shanks it.

It's no surprise that, as leaders, we can also sometimes forget the basics. The basics of our "sport" involve meeting employees' three intellectual needs:

1. Achievement

2. Autonomy

3. Mastery

> "Thought, not money, is the real business capital."
>
> – Harvey S. Firestone
> Founder, Firestone Tire &
> Rubber Company

When you fulfill these needs, you create a self-reinforcing cycle of improvement, growth and high performance for your team. The mind is a muscle. It must be exercised or it will weaken. Engaging the mind is a form of mental exercise – it strengthens your employees' ability to perform. Engage their minds and watch their performance grow!

So let's take a detailed look at the three intellectual needs and how you can fulfill them.

Achievement

The need to achieve is one of the more visible needs in our society. It fuels performance in the worlds of sports, music, politics, media and certainly, business. We all have a need to achieve. At one level or another, everyone wants to succeed at something.

An unfulfilled need for achievement leads to frustration, disappointment and a decreased sense of self-worth. These are not feelings you want your employees experiencing, and you definitely don't want the reduced productivity that accompanies them. You can use two simple strategies to help fulfill your employees' need for achievement: *eliminate barriers* and *define crystal clear goals*.

Eliminating barriers to achievement is one of the most powerful ways to engage your team. Employees want to achieve results – for themselves, for the team and for you. In fact, the human need for achievement is so strong that, for the most part, all you need to do as a leader is get out of the way! In other words, *make it easy for your employees to succeed.* This is not about lowering your standards. Making it easy for employees to succeed means eliminating barriers so their basic need to achieve can be fulfilled. Some common barriers to employee achievement that leaders can control include: insufficient materials, equipment or tools; lack of authority to accomplish goals; slow or unclear decision-making processes; and undefined goals. These barriers choke an employee's need for achievement rather than fulfill it.

So what can you do to eliminate barriers to achievement? Following are a few actions you can take. In parentheses are some typical responses your employees will have when their need for achievement is met. Whether or not you hear these responses, they will be expressed

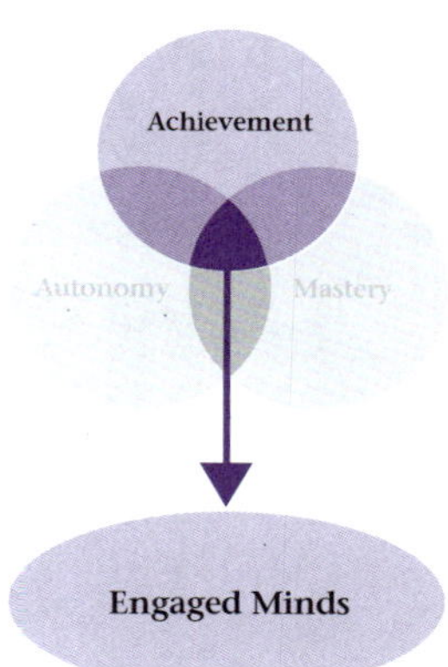

somehow, and they represent the seeds of intellectual engagement.

- ◆ **Be a resource provider.** Ensure your employees have the necessary materials, equipment and resources to achieve their goals. (*"Now I can focus on what's really important – performing."*)

- ◆ **Match authority to responsibility**. Give employees the authority they need to achieve the results for which you will hold them accountable. (*"I am in control of my destiny at work."*)

- ◆ **Be decisive.** Use the best available information and your intuition to provide definite and timely decisions for employees. Analysis paralysis is the enemy of achievement. (*"I'm not waiting on anyone except me, so I need to keep moving. I have commitments to keep!"*)

The second strategy for meeting the achievement need is to **define crystal clear goals and then keep employees focused on those goals.** To illustrate the importance of staying focused, consider two sources of energy: the sun and a laser. The sun is a powerful source of energy. It showers the earth with billions of kilowatts of energy every hour. Yet with minimal protection, say a hat and some sunscreen, you can bask in the sunlight for hours with few negative effects. On the other hand, a laser uses a weak source of energy and *focuses* it in a cohesive stream of light, producing intense heat and power. With a laser, you can drill a hole in a diamond or defeat a cancer. That's the power of focus!

It works the same for your employees. Clear goals require less energy to yield greater results because your employees' efforts are laser-like. Clear goals make it easier for

> "What you get by achieving your goals is not as important as what you become by achieving your goals."
>
> – Zig Ziglar
> Author and Speaker

employees to achieve because they can better prioritize their time and energy to focus on things that are important to your team's success.

If clearly defined goals are so powerful and support employees' need to achieve, why do so many leaders struggle with diffused employee efforts? The primary reason is today's change-intensive, information-loaded business world. This type of environment creates so many distractions, it's hard for employees (and leaders) to stay focused on their goals. These distractions steal time and energy and can quickly undermine your employees' efforts to achieve.

I recently read this saying on a poster: "When winds of change blow hard enough, even the most trivial of objects can become deadly projectiles." Invest the time to define and continually reinforce employees' goals to help them see clearly through the winds of change and achieve!

When you take action to support your employees in their quest for achievement, you take a big step toward engaging their minds and improving their performance.

Fulfilling the Need

Key strategies to fulfill your employees' need for *Achievement*:

✓ Eliminate barriers to achievement.

✓ Define crystal clear goals so employees will know when they have achieved them.

What is **one action you can take** to more effectively meet this need?

____

____

____

Autonomy

While achievement focuses on the *outcome* of your employees' work, autonomy focuses on the *process* of getting work done. Engaging leaders give their teams the freedom, or autonomy, to determine the best way to perform their jobs. These leaders realize that employees have a basic need to "own" or control how they accomplish their work.

The first strategy to fulfill this need is to *involve your employees* in defining and improving their work processes. Clearly defined processes are critical to any efficient operation. Even in the most routine jobs, you can still get input from employees about ways to make improvements. When you give team members the appropriate level of autonomy, you engage their minds. The benefit to you? **People support what they help create.** When employees support the process, they are much more likely to give discretionary effort.

Giving employees control over their work is not always intuitive or comfortable for leaders. It requires having trust in your team. Autonomy is generally more important than doing it "the way the boss said to do it." What's the risk of not providing autonomy? Employees basically become robots – they give you their hands and feet, but not their minds and hearts.

Toyota does a great job of involving employees and fulfilling their need for autonomy. Toyota employees are required to submit two suggestions per month that they can implement themselves or with a teammate – in other words, something the employee can control. As a result, Toyota receives over 3 million employee suggestions for improvement each year. More impressively, 80% of these actually get implemented! Even though many of

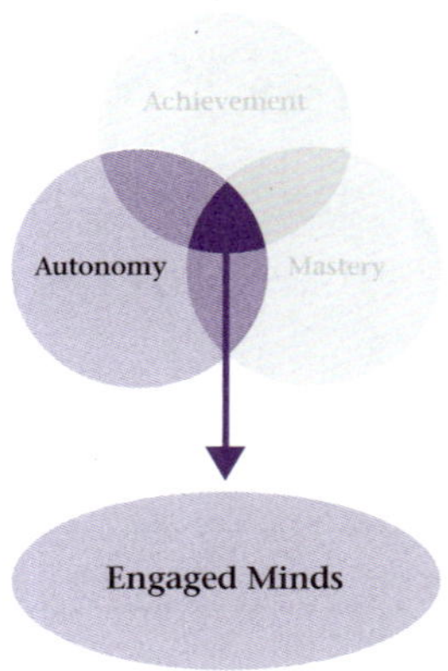

Toyota's employees perform repetitive manufacturing jobs, this approach sends a strong message that employees have control over their work processes. What kind of impact would this approach to autonomy have in your organization?

The second key strategy to fulfilling the need for autonomy is to *set clear boundaries*. Jeff Immelt is Chief Executive Officer at General Electric. One of his leadership tips is: Manage by setting boundaries, with freedom in the middle (in other words, give your employees autonomy). Immelt says, "The boundaries are commitment, passion, trust and teamwork. Within those boundaries, there's plenty of freedom."

Determine the appropriate boundaries for your team. Your organizational values can give you a hint as to what these boundaries should be (e.g., teamwork, innovation, mutual respect, customer focus, open communication, fact-based decision making, etc.). These boundaries will help you define the playing field within which employees can use their skills and creativity to get work done.

> "If you put fences around people, you get sheep."
>
> – William McKnight
> Former CEO, 3M

When you give team members autonomy, they take personal pride in their work and will:

- identify improvements you likely would not (they are closer to the work and the customer);

- use their discretionary time and effort to measure and monitor their own processes (like business owners, they will demonstrate similar efforts as owners of their processes);

♦ increase quality and quantity of output (they will feel a sense of accountability to themselves and to their team);

♦ see a clear connection between their work and the goals of the team (true process owners ask, "How does this process affect our team and our customers?").

Involve employees in improving their work processes and set clear boundaries, then you will engage their minds and be on your way to Passionate Performance!

Fulfilling the Need

Key strategies to fulfill your employees' need for *Autonomy*:

✓ When identifying improvements to work processes, focus on those that employees can implement themselves.

✓ Set broad yet clear boundaries for performance and then let your employees determine the best methods to achieve their goals.

What is **one action you can take** to more effectively meet this need?

____

____

____

Mastery

One of the strongest intellectual drives people have is to do something well – to master something. We are born with this need. Consider a baby who is learning to walk. Despite countless trips, stumbles, bumps and bruises, a baby's need to master the skill of walking remains strong until s/he can do it effortlessly. In the workplace, mastery is about being competent in a given position. A single role can require different types of knowledge and skills. For example, one job could require knowledge of your industry's supply chain, competitive pricing strategies and financial metrics, and also skills in project management, negotiation, sales and written communication.

Did you know the average person possesses between 500 and 700 different skills and abilities? An engaging leader helps employees develop and master the specific skills required for their jobs. When employees feel they have mastered their jobs, their performance will skyrocket. Two key strategies for meeting the mastery need are *fit* and *learning*.

Finding a good fit between an employee's natural abilities and interests and the requirements of the job is crucial to meeting the mastery need. Just as land developers look for the "highest and best use" of their land to maximize the return on their investment, engaging leaders view themselves as people developers. They look for the highest and best use of their employees by thoughtfully matching people to positions. This matching process is the single best predictor of how well the mastery need will be met. If you don't match the employee and the role correctly, you're stacking the odds against the employee mastering that role.

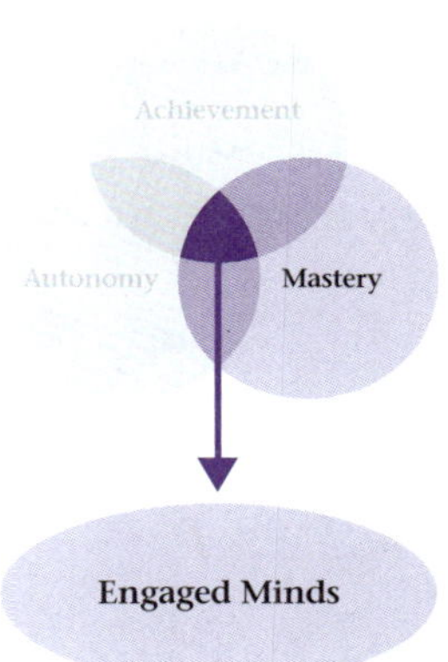

Today's fast-paced, efficiency-minded organizations make it challenging to always ensure a good fit. For example, as companies continue to do more work with fewer people, it's common to find employees picking up the slack for positions that have been eliminated. If personnel reductions aren't executed carefully, the remaining employees can find themselves *under*employed – consumed by "leftover" tasks that drain their time but don't tap their minds. This starts a cycle of "lowest and worst use" of talent. The result is a poor fit between the person and the position that frequently creates a downward spiral of self-doubt, anxiety and frustration. If you've ever experienced this, you know it feels more like misery than mastery.

To prevent this cycle of "lowest and worst use" and the resulting decline in performance, carefully design the work on your team. Consider the following:

- Combine tasks that require similar skill levels so you can more easily match the person's skills to the position's requirements.

- Automate repetitive tasks. Remember, you're trying to engage, not disengage, employees' minds.

- Streamline inefficient processes and eliminate redundant tasks that prevent employees from building mastery in the critical parts of their jobs.

- Outsource tasks that require significant effort but have little impact on the organization.

Learning is the second strategy for meeting the mastery need. **When you invest in a mind, you engage it.** Mastery is not built in chunks. It's a gradual process of layering. So create a rich, multi-layered learning environment for your team. Use a variety of learning sources – special projects, cross-functional assignments, presentations to management and training colleagues (the best test of learning is to be able to teach someone else). Layer on the experiences to build mastery.

> "In teaching others, we teach ourselves."
>
> – Proverb

Although some learning for mastery requires a financial investment (e.g., seminars, professional memberships, publications), the best return is generated from an investment of your time and energy. There are few better places to spend your leadership resources than on building your employees' mastery. Remember – successful leaders achieve results *through* others. Your employees' mastery gets *you* results.

The most important source of learning for your employees is YOU! **An engaging leader is a coach.** Share your experiences. There are lessons to be found in everything your team does. Look for opportunities in: post-project reviews, customer meetings, conflicts with other departments, changes in priorities, miscommunications and mistakes. Yes, mistakes. The truth is that good judgment comes from experience, and a lot of that comes from bad judgment. Seize all of these opportunities to coach your employees toward mastery.

Challenge your employees in every way, every day. They will master their jobs. You will engage their minds and elevate your team's performance.

Fulfilling the Need

Key strategies to fulfill your employees' need for *Mastery*:

✓ Ensure a good fit between people and positions to get the "highest and best use" of your employees' skills.

✓ Seize teachable moments to coach your employees and pass along your own mastery.

What is **one action you can take** to more effectively meet this need?

____

____

____

Engage their **MINDS**
to build *Performance*,

Engage their *HEARTS*
to create *Passion*...

then **conquer the competition** with

PASSIONATE PERFORMANCE.

"It's not the size of the man, but the size of his heart that matters."

– Evander Holyfield
Three-time World
Heavyweight Boxing Champion

Engaging
the Heart

Engaging the heart tends to be more challenging for leaders than engaging the mind. It's the softer side of leadership, but it's often harder to get your hands around. Traditional leadership development programs don't emphasize the skills necessary to engage employees' hearts, and many organizations don't reinforce these skills with their leaders. As a result, many leaders tend to be less comfortable with this side of engagement because they simply have never learned how or what to do. Emotional engagement creates an advantage that is very difficult for your competitors to duplicate, so it's worth learning to do well.

The heart represents the emotional side of people that is based on connections. This side requires the *art* of leadership that focuses on relationships. **Engaging the heart creates passion.**

Although we might like to think otherwise, the truth is that we live in a world driven by emotional decisions. Remember that 70% of customers' buying decisions are based on human interactions. Likewise, employees are primarily driven by emotional and personal considerations. When people go to work, they don't leave their hearts at home. We may live in a high-tech world, but leadership is still a high-touch job.

How often do you hear people speak with envy about companies with "real heart" – companies like The Container Store, Southwest Airlines, Harley-Davidson, Enterprise Rent-A-Car and Chick-fil-A? Outsiders are constantly looking for their "secrets" to success. The secret lies in the hearts of their employees. These companies have created connected teams and, as a result, have built dominant businesses.

If you're going to engage your employees' hearts, you must first meet their basic emotional needs:

1. Purpose

2. Intimacy

3. Appreciation

When you fulfill these needs, you create self-reinforcing connections – connections between your employees and you, between their work and their purpose, and between each other. These connections establish strong, intangible relationships that yield amazing tangible results. Engage employees' hearts and watch their passion grow!

Let's take a closer look at each of these three emotional needs and discover how you can meet each one.

We are employed

by organizations,

but we work

for people.

Purpose

All of us are in search of a clear and driving purpose for our lives; we want to contribute to something bigger than ourselves. The workplace offers a great opportunity for people to connect with a purpose. The reality is that people care less about working for a company and much more about working for a compelling cause. Without a purpose, your employees are just putting in time. Their minds might be engaged, but their hearts will not be. A team without a purpose is a team without passion. Your team members may achieve short-term results, but they won't have the heart to go the distance.

The first strategy to satisfy this basic need is to *give employees a compelling purpose and then help them connect with it emotionally.* Do a little "LBWA" – Leadership **B**y **W**alking Around. Take a close look at what your employees are doing day in and day out. You might find that their hearts are much bigger than their jobs. Get team members inspired about a cause, and their hearts will follow. **A purpose is your team's bridge to a brighter tomorrow…and you have to build it!**

A compelling purpose is *not* a project goal, financial target or strategic plan. Your employees won't get emotionally charged about a "10% net profit," "20% return on investment" or "30% increase in market share." A compelling purpose is a reason to be excited about getting up and going to work every day. Remember, now we're talking about the emotional side of engagement.

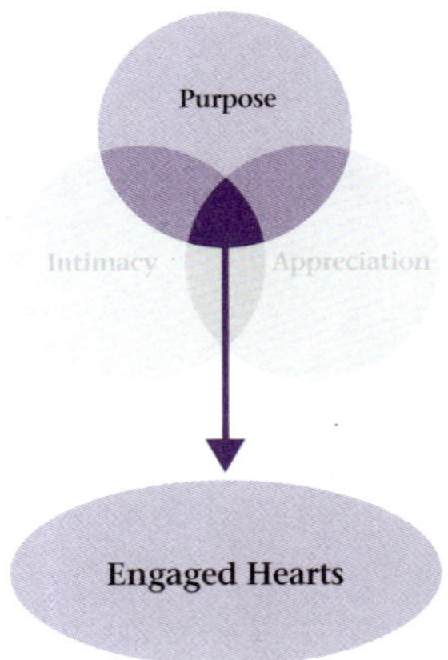

A purpose can come in all varieties – perhaps it is to help others, to make the world a better place, to innovate or to win. For example, Disney's purpose is "to make dreams come true." Coke worked diligently to develop its purpose: to put a Coke within reach of every person on Earth. Pepsi's purpose is to "beat Coke!" Your organization's real purpose may not be apparent at first glance. For instance, a company that distributes building products to homebuilders may not seem to have a compelling cause; but a deeper look reveals that they "help make the American dream a reality." That's a cause worth working for!

Your team should also have a purpose. It might simply be to support the purpose of the organization. If so, help your employees make a strong emotional connection between their individual roles and the organization's purpose.

Don't wait for your organization to communicate a purpose that your team can latch onto. Take the initiative now to engage the hearts of your employees so they will develop a passion for their work. No matter how large or small your team, define a compelling purpose. Be bold. Step back and look at the big picture. Think of how your team improves life for others. Your purpose should answer the question, "What difference are we making?" Your answer should stir your emotions.

> "It's not enough to be busy. The question is, what are we busy about?"
>
> – Henry David Thoreau
> Poet and Naturalist

For example, a customer call center may have a purpose to brighten the day of each and every caller. An information technology department's cause could be to improve personal productivity. For a purchasing department, it might be to ensure that all company products are made with the best raw materials available.

To maximize your employees' passion, fully engage their hearts by asking them how their jobs relate to your team's purpose. Some questions you might pose include:

- "How does our purpose make you feel?" (If you hear responses like *proud, important, connected, helpful* or *like a winner*, you're on the right track.)

- "Does our purpose make you look at your job differently?"

- "Do our roles, procedures, resources, skills and priorities support our ability to achieve our purpose?"

- "What can you change or do differently to better support our purpose?"

- "What can I change or do differently to better support our purpose?"

Once employees see a clear connection between their role and their purpose, the next strategy is to *help them stay focused on that purpose*. It's far too easy to become preoccupied with activity for activity's sake. We can turn into human "doings" instead of human beings. Without a daily laser-like focus on your team's purpose, employees can get caught up in their *activity* ("I am really busy") instead of their *productivity* ("I am working toward our purpose").

Engaging leaders help their team members prioritize so they can say "Yes" to those tasks that directly support the team's purpose and "No" to other tasks. **Your employees' time and energy are precious resources** – if they're spent on one task, they cannot be spent on another.

Give employees a purpose, and you fill their hearts with passion. They won't just be engaged; they'll be in overdrive!

Fulfilling the Need

Key strategies to fulfill your employees' need for *Purpose:*

✓ Create a compelling purpose and then help employees see the connection between that purpose and their roles.

✓ Stay focused on activities that directly support your team's purpose.

What is **one action you can take** to more effectively meet this need?

____

____

____

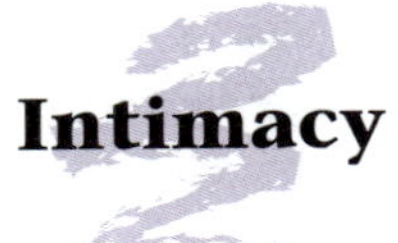

Intimacy

Intimacy makes people feel connected. It's a basic human emotional need to belong, to not be alone. At work, a need for intimacy means feeling like part of a team and being connected to those around us. When this need goes unmet, employees feel alone and disconnected. They become just a set of hands punching a clock. They leave their hearts at home – they disengage.

Fulfilling the need for intimacy is about building relationships and close connections. Your team should be the focal point for developing these connections, and there are two strategies you can use to accomplish this: *maintain smallness* and *create rituals.*

As organizations grow, more layers naturally appear between the customer and the top executive. This expanding hierarchy inhibits a team's speed, responsiveness and real-time understanding of customer needs. In addition, as teams expand, employees may find it harder to keep their fingers on the pulse of the customer. Smaller teams combat these natural tendencies. Close connections are more likely to be sustained on smaller teams. Small teams allow for more intimacy with customers (internal and external). Microsoft keeps its development teams around 12 members for this very reason. To foster closer connections with customers, keep your teams small.

Small teams also facilitate deeper relationships within the team. People want to feel like they have "family" at work. The more your employees feel family-like emotional attachments with co-workers, the more emotionally engaged they will be. They will help each other and take care of each other at work…and often beyond work. Did you know that an employee's co-workers and immediate supervisor dictate 90% of

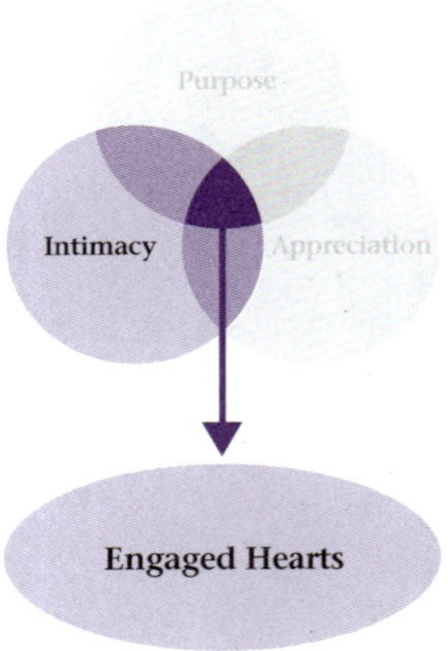

how that employee will relate to and feel about the organization? This is because the smallest team is where the closest relationships are developed. Even large, worldwide organizations depend on local leaders to build connections, foster intimacy and engage employees. The corporate office actually rides the coattails of local leaders' relationships with their teams.

When employees form close connections with one another, they become passionate about their work. They go above and beyond for each other and for the team. Let me share an illustration of this.

Not long ago, I was walking near the receiving dock at the back of a store location for a national retailer. I watched as an entry-level clerk in his early twenties abruptly stopped an empty truck before it left the dock. He quickly grabbed a broom, hopped into the back of the truck, gave it a good once-over with the broom, and then motioned the driver to go ahead. After the truck pulled away, I walked past him and jokingly said, "Nice jump back there!" He replied, "Well, I'm done with my shift, but I wanted to make sure the truck was cleaned up. It saves Jeff time back at the warehouse when he picks up another load. Jeff is on my service team, and he's had a pretty hectic schedule lately. I just wanted to help him out. No big deal." Now that's the power of connected, engaged teams!

The second strategy for meeting the intimacy need is to create rituals. Engaging leaders do what other leaders might consider to be corny. These leaders make it a priority to **establish rituals and "traditions" that connect employees to each other and to the customer.** The purpose is to foster intimacy, belonging and fun. And I can assure you that their employees certainly do not think these events are corny. Try some of these rituals with your team:

- Celebrate employee birthdays and special occasions.
- Create team cheers.
- Coordinate social events and gatherings.
- Post photos of team members and customers.

Engaging employees' hearts is a personal matter. Maintaining small teams and creating rituals help fulfill your team's need for intimacy. If employees aren't close with their team members, it's unlikely your organization will be close with its customers.

Fulfilling the Need

Key strategies to fulfill your employees' need for *Intimacy*:

✓ Maintain small teams to keep employees connected with their customers and each other.

✓ Create rituals and celebrations to facilitate a sense of belonging and an atmosphere of fun.

What is **one action you can take** to more effectively meet this need?

____

____

____

Appreciation

William James, the father of psychology, stated that a fundamental human need is to be appreciated. This idea is supported by many studies that show the number one need expressed by employees is to *feel fully appreciated for their work*. Although leaders widely recognize the need for employee appreciation, it tends to be a blind spot for many leaders. In other words, **leaders generally believe they are much more appreciative of their employees than their employees think they are.**

Employees subconsciously "add up" their contributions and compare that to the appreciation they receive for their work. Then they ask the question, "Is the difference positive, negative or in balance?" If they perceive that the appreciation you express is less than their contributions, they will be on the fast track to disengagement. To engage their hearts, your appreciation must equal, or ideally exceed, their level of contribution.

Engaging leaders utilize two strategies to fulfill the need for appreciation:

1. Appreciate contributions
2. Appreciate the person

Appreciate employees' contributions by proactively looking for opportunities to acknowledge their efforts and results. **Catch people doing something good…and do it often!** Although cash reinforcements are one way to acknowledge contributions, they tend to have limited potential for engaging employees' hearts. On the other hand, *non*-cash appreciation is more powerful and longer lasting. Why? Because it's personal – it builds relationships and connections with employees. As a result,

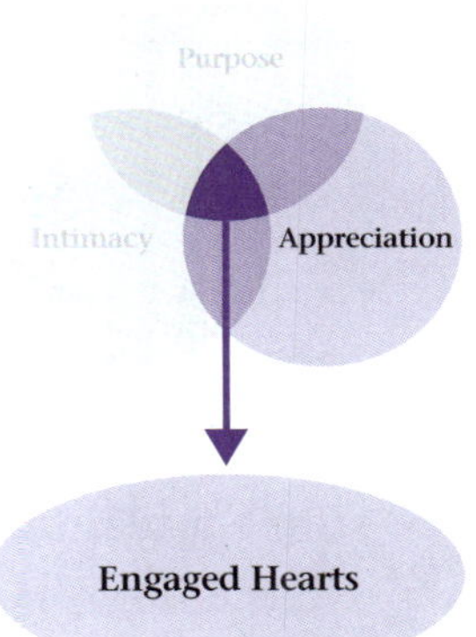

it engages the heart of the recipient. This is basic psychology –
reinforce those behaviors that you want to see more of.

> "People will forget what you said. People will even forget what you did. But people will never forget how you made them feel."
>
> – Unknown

The good news is that leaders have complete control over this type of personal appreciation. No budget limitations here – there are literally thousands of ways to appreciate your employees' contributions at little or no cost. Learn to effectively express your appreciation for employees' efforts. Appreciation should be memorable, sincere, motivating and meaningful to the employee, and it should provide acknowledgement with peers. Here are some ways you can meet employees' need for appreciation and engage their hearts:

♦ Say "Thank you!" – an all-too-obvious yet highly underused form of appreciation.

♦ Allow employees to present their work to your boss. This is a great way to engage employees, and it also shows your boss what kind of leader you are.

♦ Offer team members a choice of projects to work on. When employees buy into a project, they will put their hearts into it.

♦ Put a sincere acknowledgement in your company or department newsletter. This takes only a few minutes of your time, but creates long-term "trophy value" for the employee.

♦ Tell an employee's story of accomplishment at a staff meeting. Stories are perceived as more interesting, meaningful, thoughtful and memorable.

♦ Take a team member to lunch to show your appreciation. Remember to do more listening than talking.

Carly Fiorina, CEO of Hewlett Packard, can certainly be considered a busy leader with many demands on her time. However, she always finds time to show her appreciation for employees who close new contracts with balloons, gifts, cakes, etc. Appreciating employee contributions is not a matter of time; it's a matter of priority.

The engaging leader also knows that appreciating *the person* is just as important as appreciating contributions. A study of over 20,000 leaders found that the most effective ones had one thing in common: They expressed a sincere interest in, and appreciation for, their employees as people. "Sincere" is the operative word here. Your motivation matters! If you acknowledge employees in hopes of getting something in return, they will see right through you.

Learn something new each day about one of your employees. Ask about family, hobbies, leisure activities, etc. You will begin to understand and appreciate them more fully. Then weave this information into your interactions with them. They will return your appreciation with passion for your leadership.

The bottom line is this: **We do more for those who appreciate us.** Appreciate your employees and you will engage their hearts!

Fulfilling the Need

Key strategies to fulfill your employees' need for *Appreciation*:

✓ Look for opportunities to show your appreciation for employee contributions.

✓ Appreciate employees as people. Learn what makes them tick.

What is **one action you can take** to more effectively meet this need?

____

____

____

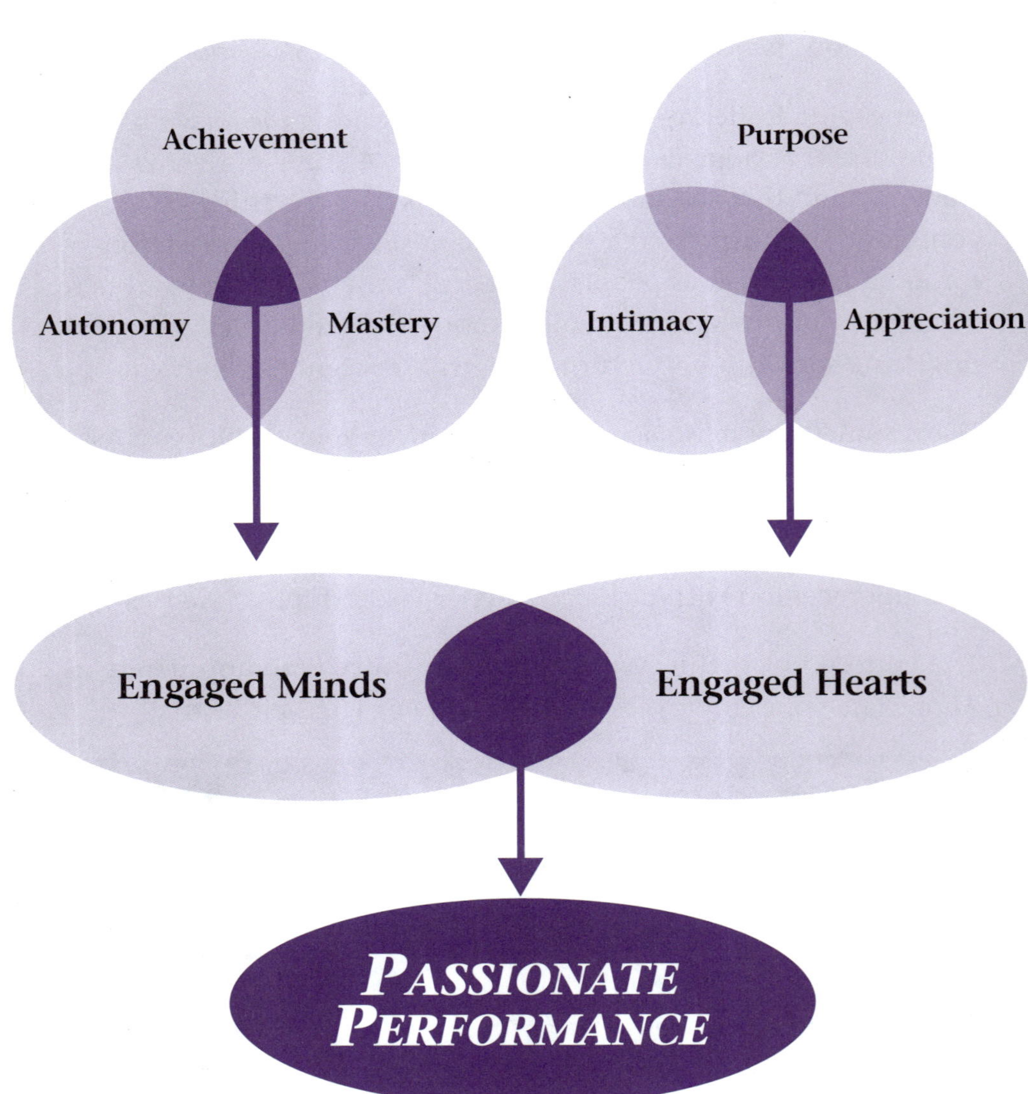

Achievement
Autonomy
Mastery
Purpose
Intimacy
Appreciation
Engaged Minds
Engaged Hearts
PASSIONATE PERFORMANCE

LEADING THE WAY

Engaging Strategies

Engaged minds build your employees' performance and engaged hearts build their passion – they go hand in hand. You ignite Passionate Performance only when all three intellectual and all three emotional needs are fulfilled and you connect minds and hearts. The chart on the next page summarizes the strategies to fulfill the six needs we have discussed. Take a moment to review them before we discuss how you can lead the way to Passionate Performance.

"Engaging leaders make good employees into better people."

– Ed Gubman
Management Consultant
and Author

Needs	Strategies
Intellectual	
Achievement	♦ Eliminate barriers to achievement. ♦ Define crystal clear goals.
Autonomy	♦ Involve employees in improving their work processes. ♦ Set broad yet clear boundaries.
Mastery	♦ Fit person to position for "highest and best use." ♦ Seize teachable moments to coach employees.
Emotional	
Purpose	♦ Connect roles to a compelling purpose. ♦ Stay focused on activities that support your purpose.
Intimacy	♦ Maintain small teams. ♦ Create and reinforce team rituals.
Appreciation	♦ Find opportunities to appreciate employees' contributions. ♦ Demonstrate a sincere interest in your employees as people. Learn what makes them tick.

Leading the way to Passionate Performance for your team is a big responsibility. As a leader, you're the only person who can engage your employees. It's not your boss's responsibility or Human Resources' – it's yours. Engaging employees is a personal matter, not a company matter.

Meeting your employees' needs and engaging them is a long-term process, and there are no shortcuts. **You need to mentally prepare for a marathon versus a sprint.** And there may be some bumps in the road. You may not see the sparks of Passionate Performance until you are well into the race and feeling weary, like you can't go on. That's usually about the time your team seems to give it all back, and you see the positive results of your efforts. It's like the "runner's high." Suddenly your team's success appears effortless – you are in the zone. Only you and your team can fully appreciate the simplicity and hard work behind your winning ways. Best of all, you leave your competition in the dust as you cruise past them.

Of course, you will never win the race if you don't *start* the race. A marathoner doesn't start a race thinking about mile 26. She starts the race thinking about the first mile, and then she takes one step at a time. You need to do the same. Passionate Performance is your ultimate goal, but you have to take one step at a time. **Start the journey by thinking about fulfilling one basic need at a time.**

Speaking of long journeys, did you know that a lunar voyage is about half a million miles roundtrip? Here's the really interesting part: More energy is spent in the first few seconds and miles of that voyage than in the remaining days and half million miles. The gravitational pull of the earth in those first miles is tremendous (probably a lot like pulling my kids away from the television on Saturday mornings!). It takes an internal thrust greater than the force of gravity and the resistance of the atmosphere to put the spacecraft into orbit. But once it's in orbit, it takes very little power to complete the rest of the voyage.

This is a powerful metaphor for describing what it takes to build new, engaging leadership habits. It can be uncomfortable and very effortful at first, and you may even feel resistance to your own "gravitational pull." But once you develop a new habit, it feels comfortable and effortless. Engaging leaders will tell you that it's well worth the initial discomfort to achieve Passionate Performance.

To get
Passionate Performance,
you must give it.

The first step in the journey is yours: **Engaging leaders start with themselves.** They ensure that they are fully engaged before they try to engage their employees. So, if you think your team's achievement is low, examine your own need for achievement. If your team's mastery is lacking, ask yourself what you can do to build your own mastery. If your team's sense of purpose seems heartless, look into the heart of your own purpose. Living as a positive example is perhaps the most powerful engagement strategy of all.

The next step is to focus on meeting your employees' needs. Go back and reread the section of this book that corresponds to the basic need you think is the biggest challenge for your team. Look at the one action you wrote down in the "Fulfilling the Need" section. Then, **commit to that action!** Here are examples of actions you might take:

- I will look for opportunities to help my employees master key skills.

- I will eliminate the primary barrier to achievement by defining clear goals with each employee.

- I will find one reason every day to recognize someone on my team.

- I will ask for suggestions for improvement at every staff meeting.

- I will implement a structured selection process to ensure a good fit between person and position.

- I will review my team's structure to ensure that all team members feel closely connected to their peers and their customers.

- I will ask my employees what changes they can make to be certain we stay focused on our purpose.

Now, **turn the one action you selected into a positive habit.** It takes 28 days of action and reinforcement to create a new habit. So stick to just one action until you're certain you've created a habit that fulfills a basic need for employees. After 28 days of disciplined effort, your new habit should require minimal effort to maintain. It will begin to be the natural way you lead.

Once your new action has truly become a habit, come back to this book. Identify another unmet need to fulfill and build another positive habit. Take baby steps to create successes upon which you and your team can build confidence and momentum. Remember, it's a long race.

Start *today* with one simple action. Then follow that up with another. You will be well on your way to meeting your employees' needs. Eventually you will achieve a "runner's high," and you will discover that you have fully engaged the minds and hearts of your employees. Everyone on your team will deliver Passionate Performance every day. *You will win the race and conquer the competition!*

Successful leaders have

successful habits.

They sacrifice today's pleasures

for tomorrow's rewards.

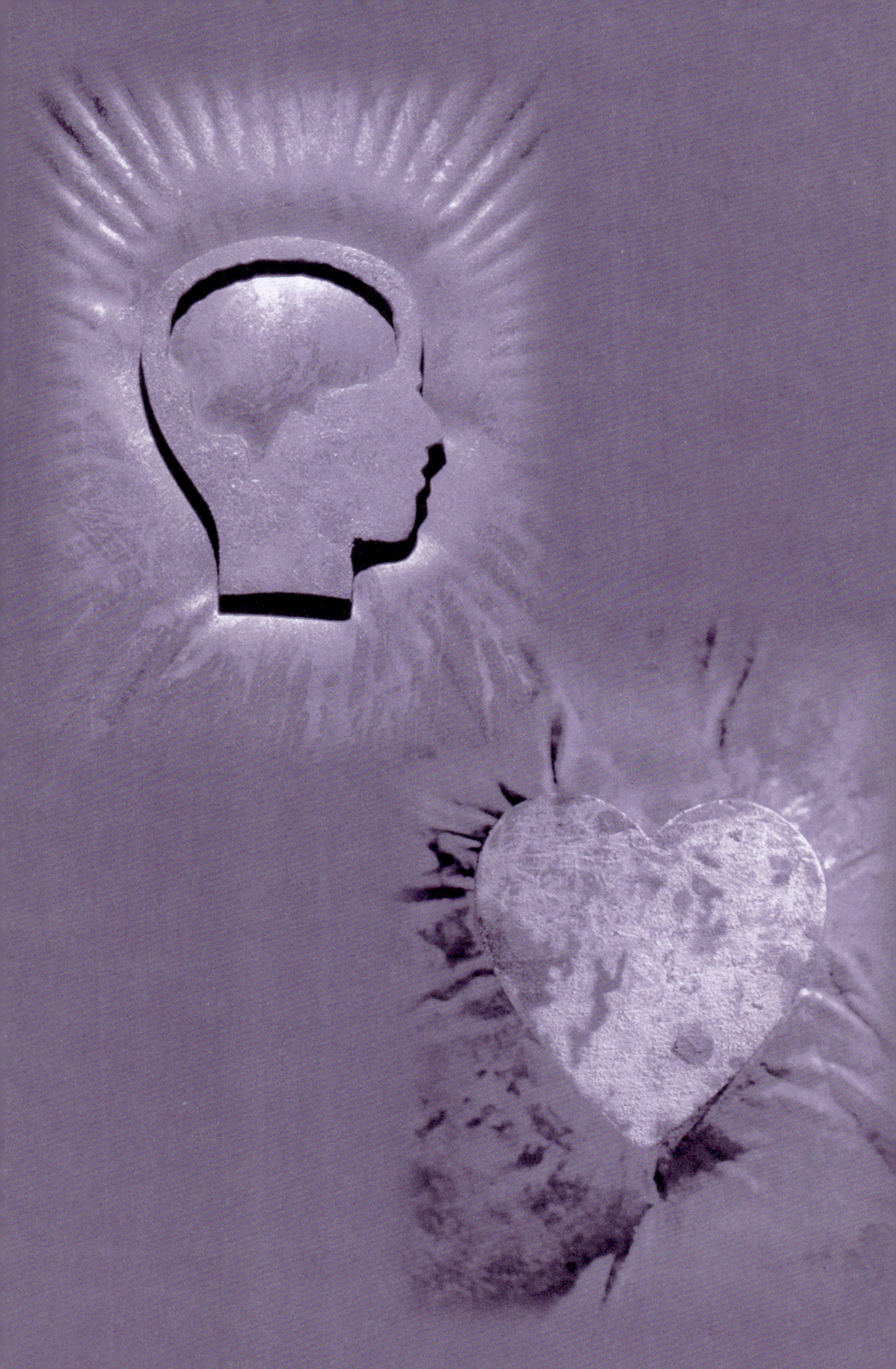

"*Empty pockets never held anyone back. Only empty heads and empty hearts can do that.*"

– Norman Vincent Peale
Author and Speaker

Seven ways to reinforce *Passionate Performance:*

1. Keynote Presentation
Invite author Lee J. Colan to ignite your team and share insights to help them become more engaging leaders.

2. Workshop
Facilitated by the author or a certified facilitator, this three- or six-hour workshop provides participants with relevant examples and simple tools they can apply immediately. Participants will create personal action plans to become more engaging leaders.

3. PowerPoint® Presentation
Introduce and reinforce the *Passionate Performance* concepts and strategies to your team with this professionally designed presentation. Use the presentation for staff, brown bag lunches or as a follow-up development tool. 48 slides plus 4 BONUS tools! $99.95

4. At-a-Glance Reminder Cards
These attractively designed, quick-reference cards summarize the key strategies for engaging your team to boost their discretionary effort. Perfect for every leader to have at their fingertips! 5" x 7" cards. Pk/10 $19.95

5. Learning Cubes
Play and learn! A great interactive way to reinforce the *Passionate Performance* message. Use them as reminders or as hands-on quick reference guides to employee engagement. Each side reveals an engaging strategy or inspirational message. Set of 10 cubes. $39.95

6. 180-degree Profile
This confidential, on-line profile assesses your team's intellectual and emotional engagement. The *Passionate Performance* profile is easy to use and provides you with valuable insights on the six critical employee needs. You receive a 20+ page, personalized profile comparing your self-assessment with assessments from up to 10 employees. $99.95.

7. Learning Reinforcement Kit
Perfect to help to drive sustained learning and performance! Kit includes one of each: *Passionate Performance* rapid-read book, interactive learning cube, At-a-Glance reminder card. $14.95/kit

Passionate Performance

Profile

Put your finger on the pulse of your employees' minds and hearts! Take this confidential, on-line profile to assess your team's engagement.

The profile provides you with valuable insights on the six critical employee needs. Your **personalized profile** will help you:

- measure the engagement of your team;

- recognize employee needs you can more effectively fulfill; and

- prioritize a plan to pursue Passionate Performance.

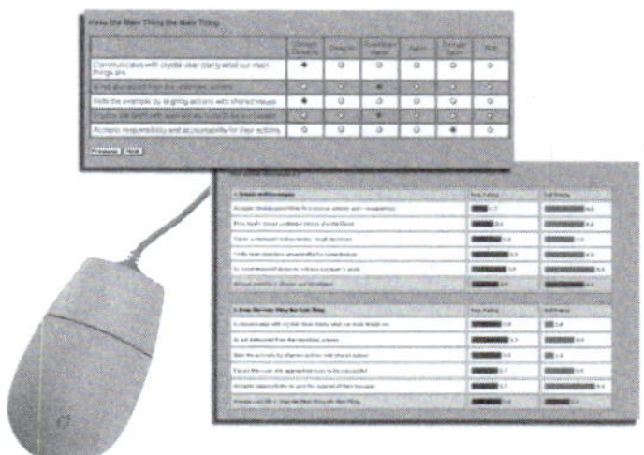

Other **Benefits** of the *Passionate Performance* Profile:

- *Confidential* – participant feedback is completely confidential.

- *On-line* – you can complete it anytime, anywhere. No need for a special meeting.

- *Easy to use* – simple, step-by-step instructions. No software or installation required.

- *Multiple perspectives* – include up to 10 people to gain a rich perspective of your team's engagement.

- *Cost effective.*

To learn more and order your *Passionate Performance* Profile, go to **www.theLgroup.com**

Reflect your organization's values with
dramatic, inspiring note cards,
framed desktop prints and posters!

Integrity ♦ Change ♦ Perseverance
Focus ♦ Courage ♦ Press On

See the entire collection at
www.CornerStoneLeadership.com

The CornerStone Perpetual Calendar, a compelling collection of quotes about leadership and life, is perfect for office desks, school and home countertops. Offering a daily dose of inspiration, this terrific calendar makes the perfect gift or motivational reward. $12.95

888.789.LEAD

www.**CornerStoneLeadership**.com

Other Management Development Resources

Power Exchange – How to Boost Accountability & Performance in Today's Workforce by Lee J. Colan is a quick read that offers practical strategies to help any leader boost accountability and performance in today's workforce. $9.95

Monday Morning Leadership is David Cottrell's best-selling book. It offers unique encouragement and direction that will help you become a better manager, employee and person. $14.95

Conquering Adversity – Six Strategies to Move You and Your Team Through Tough Times is practical guide to help people and organizations deal with the unexpected and move forward through adversity. $14.95

Management Insights explores the myths and realities of management. It provides insight into how you can become a successful manager. $14.95

136 Effective Presentation Tips is a powerful handbook providing 136 practical, easy-to-use tips to make every presentation a success. $9.95

Back to Basics …Tried and True Solutions for Today's Leaders 32 of the best "basic" ideas and strategies that are the core of an organization's success. $9.95

175 Ways to Get More Done in Less Time has 175 excellent tips and techniques to help you get things done faster … and better. $9.95

The Manager's Communication Handbook is a powerful handbook that helps you connect with employees and create the understanding, support and acceptance critical to your success. $9.95

Ethics 4 Everyone is a real world guide for corporate leaders on how to lead with integrity. Following these guidelines will help your company win the right way. $9.95

180 Ways to Walk the Recognition Talk is packed full with proven ideas and techniques that will help you provide recognition to your people more often and more effectively. $9.95

The Manager's Coaching Handbook is a practical guide to improving performance from your superstars, middle stars and falling stars. $9.95

The CornerStone Perpetual Calendar, a compelling collection of quotes about leadership and life, is perfect for office desks, school and home countertops. $12.95

The CornerStone Leadership Collection of Cards is designed to make it easy for you to show appreciation for your team, clients and friends. The awesome photography and your personal message written inside will create a lasting impact. Pack of 30 (6 styles/5 each) $34.95
Posters also available.

Visit www.CornerStoneLeadership.com for additional books and resources.

Order Form

1-99 copies $9.95   100-499 copies $8.95   500+ copies $7.95

Passionate Performance   _____ copies X _______   = $_______

Passionate Performance Companion Resources

PowerPoint® Presentation (downloadable)   _____ copies X $99.95   = $_______
Learning Cubes (set/10)   _____ set(s) X $39.95   = $_______
At-a-Glance Reminder Cards (pk/10)   _____ pack(s) X $19.95 = $_______

Additional Leadership Development Resources

The ULTIMATE ADVANTAGE Series   _____ set(s) X $27.95   = $_______
(Includes *Sticking to It, Passionate Performance &*
Orchestrating Attitude)

Management Development Package   _____ pack(s) X $179.95 = $_______
(Includes one copy of *Passionate Performance* and
all products listed on previous page)

Other Books

_______________________________   _____ copies X _______   = $_______

_______________________________   _____ copies X _______   = $_______

_______________________________   _____ copies X _______   = $_______

Shipping & Handling $_______

Subtotal $_______

Sales Tax (8.25%-TX Only) $_______

Total (U.S. Dollars Only) $_______

Shipping and Handling Charges

Total $ Amount	Up to $50	$51-$99	$100-$249	$250-$1199	$1200-$2999	$3000+
Charge	$6	$9	$16	$30	$80	$125

Name _______________________________ Job Title _______________________

Organization _______________________ Phone ___________________________

Shipping Address ____________________ Fax _____________________________

Billing Address _____________________ Email ___________________________
(required when ordering PowerPoint® Presentation)

City _______________________ State ___________ ZIP _______________

❑ Please invoice (Orders over $200) Purchase Order Number (if applicable) _______________

Charge Your Order: ❑ MasterCard   ❑ Visa   ❑ American Express

Credit Card Number _______________________ Exp. Date _______________

Signature _______________________________

❑ Check Enclosed (Payable to: CornerStone Leadership)

Phone 888.789.5323

Fax 972.274.2884   **www.CornerStoneLeadership**.com

Mail
P.O. Box 764087
Dallas, TX 75376

Published by

Leadership Institute